Esther:
The Role of a Lifetime

A Bible Study for Teen Girls

LifeWay Press®
Nashville, TN

ISBN: 978-1-4158-6604-7
Item 005168145

This book is a resource in the "Ministry" category
of the Christian Growth Study Plan. Course CG-1426
Dewey Decimal classification Number: 222.9
Subject Heading: PROVIDENCE AND GOVERNMENT OF GOD
\ BIBLE. O.T. ESTHER \ ESTHER, QUEEN

Printed in the United States of America

Student Ministry Publishing
LifeWay Church Resources
One LifeWay Plaza
Nashville, Tennessee 37234-0174

We believe that the Bible has God for its author; salvation for its end;
and truth, without any mixture of error, for its matter and that all Scripture
is totally true and trustworthy. The 2000 statement of *The Baptist Faith
and Message* is our doctrinal guideline.

Cover Illustration by Mary Lynn Blasutta

Table of Contents

About the Author

PAM GIBBS serves as the Girls Ministry Specialist at LifeWay Christian Resources, although her coworkers know she's actually the resident practical joker. She has worked at LifeWay since 1999.

Pam is a native Texan who became a Christian at youth camp at age 13. She began working in youth ministry at age 19. She graduated from Wayland Baptist University (where she was a disc jockey and even took a class in roller skating) before getting her Master's of Divinity degree at Southwestern Baptist Theological Seminary.

After moving to Nashville, she went on a blind date with a high school teacher and coach named Jim, whom she married in 2002. Jim and Pam adopted a baby girl, Kaitlyn, from Guatemala in 2006. Pam's other love is chocolate, especially dark chocolate. She also loves to lose herself in a good book or movie and is obsessed with playing games on Facebook®. Pam loves to be on the go and enjoys traveling for work. Her dream is to scuba dive off the Great Barrier Reef in Australia, but she'll need to learn how to scuba dive first!

Pam's favorite verse is Psalm 46:10: "Be still, and know that I am God." And she takes that verse to heart. She has led seminars and written articles about the practice of contemplative prayer and other ways of drawing closer to God, and any one of the women she's mentored will tell you that she is one of the most genuine Christians you will meet. She's not afraid to be real, a quality that will hopefully be evident to you as you read this book.

Special Thanks

We would like to thank the following girls
for their help in designing this Bible study. You rock!

Bethany Aycock ✽ Ashton Daniel ✽ Lisa Herod
Becca Herod ✽ Hannah Wakefield

This book is dedicated

in loving memory

to

Stephanie Lynn Wright

September 26, 1974 – December 23, 2005

Stephanie was a part of every one of our lives, even those of you who never knew her. To us at LifeWay, she was a beloved friend, coworker, event coordinator, student, teacher, mentor, counselor, and a true worshiper. To you, she was your voice. We really wish you had known our friend Stephanie. Long before any resource had been published for teen girls, she was passionate about our ministry to you because she knew what it was like to be where you are. She understood what it was like to be a young woman seeking the Lord in the midst of a chaotic and crazy world.

On December 23, 2005, Stephanie was involved in a fatal car accident. She was only 31. While we still mourn her absence, it is her life's touch that we remember so fondly. Stephanie lived a captivating and passionate life. Her life richly blessed so many individuals in many different ways. She was a student who possessed a hunger for studying God's Word that we all longed for. She was a devoted friend to countless people—investing her time, energy, and wisdom in so many.

Stephanie always closed her letters and e-mails with "In HIS Hands." In this book, we celebrate and honor the truth that Stephanie is truly in God's hands.

Introduction

EVERYONE LOVES A GOOD STORY. WE'RE DRAWN INTO "ONCE UPON A TIME" FOLLOWED BY PASSION, INTRIGUE, CONFLICT, AND DANGER. WE LOVE IT WHEN THE GOOD GUY WINS AND THEY ALL LIVE HAPPILY EVER AFTER. WE GET SWEPT AWAY BY CAR CHASES, LOVE TRIANGLES, MISTAKEN IDENTITY, AND THE TRIUMPH OF GOOD OVER EVIL.

The story of Esther can sweep you away, too (except there's no car chase). There is a king and queen. There is a good guy (and girl!) and a bad guy. A murder plot. A beauty pageant. You'll find suspicion. Intrigue. Danger. And a surprise ending.

While this story focuses on Esther, you'll quickly discover that in some places in the plot, she quietly fades into the background. Like a good storyteller, the writer of Esther wove together the actions and attitudes of many different people. You can learn from all of the characters in one way or another. Some are great models for you to follow. Others are great examples of what NOT to do.

To help you keep track of the characters, check out the diagram at the bottom of this page. You can refer back to it if you forget who's who.

You'll also discover there is no mention of God anywhere in this book. Nothing about prayer. Or the Ten Commandments. Or anything else remotely "churchy." In fact, the Book of Esther was almost excluded from the Bible for that very reason. Keep in mind, though, that just because God's name isn't mentioned doesn't mean that God isn't present. As you'll quickly learn, one of the main themes of Esther is God's providence and His presence in every event. God is silently at work behind the scenes, working out everything to His end and for His glory.

By the end of this study, you'll be swept up in a story of one woman who chooses the road of courage and action, changing the course of her nation's history even though she could have been killed. Hopefully, you will see a bit of Esther in yourself, too.

God's silence should never be equated with God's absence.

HAMAN
King Ahasuerus'
right-hand man;
Mordecai's adversary

VASHTI
Queen of Persia
in Chapter 1

AHASUERUS
King of Persia
(also known as Xerxes)

MORDECAI
Esther's cousin
and adopted father;
servant of the king

ESTHER
Mordecai's cousin;
Ahasuerus' wife
(after chapter 1)

One Man's Haste

ONE DAY IN HIGH SCHOOL, THE ADMINISTRATION PULLED THE JUNIOR CLASS INTO THE GYM SO THE LOCAL JEWELRY COMPANY COULD DISTRIBUTE INFORMATION ABOUT CLASS RINGS. THE ASSEMBLY WAS BORING, AND I WAS IN A RUSH TO GET OUT OF SCHOOL AND MOVE ONTO SOMETHING MORE IMPORTANT (PROBABLY MY BOYFRIEND).

Thinking I would beat the rush once we were dismissed, I decided to hop down onto the gym floor from a few rows up in the bleachers. In a brilliant display of athletic coordination, my heel caught on a row of seats below me, sending my whole body backwards. The back of my head landed on another row of seats, blinding me momentarily with pain. There I was, half-conscious and splayed out in front of everyone. I instantly became the topic of conversation as the dumb girl who fell. In my haste, I made a very poor decision, and boy, did I pay for it!

What about you? Do you get in a hurry? Take the quiz on the next page to find out.

Quiz:
Do You Hurry?

Check out the quiz below to determine whether or not you are a hurry-er! *True or False:*

1. (T) (F) *Thirty minutes is too long to wait for a table at a restaurant.*
2. (T) (F) *You get irritated if a friend takes too long to text you back.*
3. (T) (F) *Waiting at red lights drives you crazy.*
4. (T) (F) *You tend to think through all the alternatives when making decisions.*
5. (T) (F) *When you shop, you buy the first pair of jeans you like instead of looking around more.*
6. (T) (F) *You can't stand commercials when you're watching TV, so you either change the channel or use your DVR to fast-forward through them.*
7. (T) (F) *When you finish a test, you turn it in only after you've double- and triple-checked your answers.*
8. (T) (F) *You can recall a bad-hair phase that resulted from a spur-of-the-moment decision you made to cut or dye your hair.*
9. (T) (F) *You look for the shortest line at the checkout counter and race in front of others to get there first.*
10. (T) (F) *You prefer to read the novel rather than watch the movie based on it.*

You probably gathered that answering "true" to most of these questions revealed a lack of patience on your part. Look specifically at questions 4, 7, and 10. If you answered all three as "False," then it's safe to assume that you do things in a hurry. Being quick and efficient is not necessarily a bad thing; sometimes, though, being hasty can cause some real problems, as you'll discover in this study. But if you answered "true" to questions 4, 7, and 10, it sounds as though you are thorough and patient. And if you have some mixture of answers to those questions, then know you're not alone in your times of impatience and haste. Wherever you stand on this quiz, take a lesson from the story of Esther. Sometimes we are called to wait patiently; other times, we must act quickly. Wisdom is the key to knowing the difference.

In this chapter, we'll meet one of the main characters in the story of Esther, a man whose hasty actions set off a chain of events that changed the lives of many people. Let's meet him now.

May I Introduce . . .

Read Esther 1:1-5.

٭ *Who is mentioned in these first few verses?*

_____

٭ *What did the king do?*

_____

_____

٭ *Why do you think he held this massive feast?*

_____

_____

_____

Ahasuerus:
uh haz yoo
EHR russ

Meet King Ahasuerus. Ruler from India to Ethiopia. Your Bible may use the name "Xerxes." Same guy. And there was no more powerful man on the planet at the time. In the third year of his reign (he reigned 21 years total), he gave a banquet. That's not so unusual. Lots of kings in the ancient world gave banquets and invited the "A list" to attend.

But did you catch how long this party lasted? 180 days. For SIX MONTHS, the king showed off his royal glory and the majesty of his kingdom. And if that weren't enough, he held another week-long banquet for the people of Susa (where he lived), and invited every person in the kingdom to attend, from the greatest to the least. No one was excluded. Can you imagine how expensive that party must have been? (If you want to read about that party, check out verses 6-9).

٭ *In your own mind, how would you picture this party? Write or draw out your thoughts on the left.*

May I Also Introduce . . .

At this point in the story, another character enters the picture. Her part is small, but her role is pivotal. Read about her in Esther 1:10-12.

* What new character do we meet?

* What did the king ask her to do?

* How did she respond?

* How do you think she felt?

* Put yourself in the king's shoes. How do you think he felt?

* How does verse 10 describe him? How might this have contributed to his emotional state?

* If you were the queen, what would you have done, knowing everything that was at stake?

The plans

of the

diligent

lead to

profit as

surely

as haste

leads to

poverty.

(Proverbs 21:5, NIV)

Vashti:
VASH tigh

Meet Queen Vashti. We don't know much about her because she makes her exit so early in the story. We do know that she gave a banquet for the women in the palace at the same time the king gave his (Esth. 1:9). On the last day of the king's banquet for the people of Susa, he was "feeling good from the wine." Translation: he was drunk. In this alcohol-induced euphoria, he decided to show off one more part of his kingdom—his wife in all her beauty! Some scholars think that King Ahasuerus wanted to show off his wife wearing her crown—and nothing else!

We may not know much about Queen Vashti, but we do learn that she was strong. She refused to be paraded around in front of a bunch of men who were probably as drunk as their king. She was strong enough to stand up against wrong being done to her, which would cost her dearly. It could have even cost her life. Luckily, she was spared.

If you think about her situation, it's not too different from that of many women today. The setting is different but the challenge is the same. Thousands of women will use their bodies to find or keep success, money, or the approval of those around them. They parade their bodies, showing everything off in order to please someone, most often a guy. Unfortunately, they do not have the same courage or self-respect as demonstrated by Queen Vashti. She had everything. Life in the palace. The finest of food, clothes, and jewelry. Servants to wait on her. Maids to clean for her. And she gave it all up to save her dignity.

And Now on Stage

Here's where the plot takes an interesting turn. The king is stuck. What is he supposed to do now? Read Esther 1:13-22.

✳ *Whom else do we meet in this story?*

_____

_____

✳ *Why did the king seek their counsel?*

_____

_____

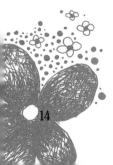

✳ *What were his advisors afraid of?*

_____

_____

_____

✳ *What mistakes do you think King Ahasuerus made in this story?*

_____

_____

_____

✳ *How did King Ahasuerus' hasty decision affect others?*

_____

_____

_____

✳ *How has a recent decision you made affected others, good or bad?*

_____

_____

_____

In these verses we meet the king's advisors. His cabinet. His right-hand help. His posse. He went to them for advice. The mighty king from the earlier verses couldn't even get his wife to do what he wanted. The situation was getting out of control, and he didn't know what to do. If he didn't respond, word would get around that the king was weak and his own wife wouldn't listen to him. Who would want to follow the leadership of a king whose own wife rejected his authority? The council of men was equally outraged by Queen Vashti's defiance against the king. What if their wives followed in Queen Vashti's footsteps? They would lose total control!

Their solution? Banish Queen Vashti. Get rid of her. Show her the door. And that's what happened. Because she treasured her dignity more than her position as queen, she kept her dignity and lost her crown. Good choice.

Introducing . . . Esther

So how does the story of the beautiful Queen Vashti and the prideful King Ahasuerus relate to Esther? Esther 2:1-4 tells us. The king's anger subsided, and he "remembered Vashti." Some versions of the Bible say that the king had "second thoughts" (The Message) about what he had done to Vashti. When the king cooled off, sobered up, and got his pride back, he began to regret his hasty decision. But his law was irrevocable. There was no way to get Vashti back. The solution? Find a new queen. Goodbye Vashti. Hello Esther. (More about that later!)

The point is this: Esther had no idea any of this was going on. At this point in the story, she did not know she would become swept up in a series of events that would change her life, all because a king wanted to show off his wife who wasn't willing. Esther was probably doing what she'd always done every day. But God, who knows all and sees all, was very much aware of what was happening. And He was working all things together. Later in the story, you'll discover how God had His hands on the situation for a much larger purpose!

A Lot in Common

Believe it or not, you and I are a lot like King Ahasuerus. OK, you probably don't run a kingdom, and you probably haven't ever hosted a feast that lasted several months. But ask yourself this: Have you ever made a decision in haste that you later regretted? Have you ever done something in the heat of the moment that you wish you could go back and change? Have you ever done anything in a hurry and paid the consequences later? Maybe you are a little more like the king than you thought!

> But the plans of the LORD stand firm forever, the purposes of his heart through all generations.
>
> (Psalm 33:11, NIV)

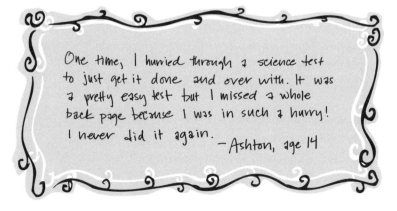

One time, I hurried through a science test to just get it done and over with. It was a pretty easy test but I missed a whole back page because I was in such a hurry! I never did it again. —Ashton, age 14

Your Turn

∗ *Each of the decisions below can be costly for you and those around you. In each box, write down some consequences you or others have faced because of these decisions.*

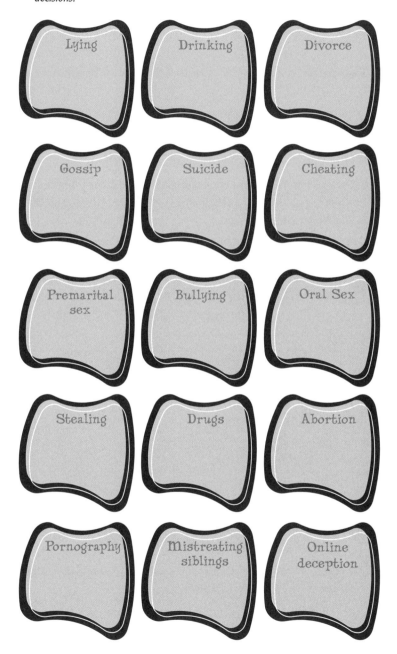

Lying

Drinking

Divorce

Gossip

Suicide

Cheating

Premarital sex

Bullying

Oral Sex

Stealing

Drugs

Abortion

Pornography

Mistreating siblings

Online deception

What can you learn from King Ahasuerus' hasty choices?

_____

_____

_____

If he could do it over again, what do you think the king would do differently?

_____

_____

Enthusiasm without knowledge is no good; haste makes mistakes.

(Proverbs 19:2, NIV)

Scripture tells us the value of not making harsh and quick responses in the heat of the moment—especially when we're angry. Nothing good happens. Keep in mind, though, that God is bigger than your mistakes and He can bring about good from the bad. You'll see that happen over and over again in the next few chapters. God is sovereign and providential over all! In other words, He sees all and knows all. He is working out everything to His end, His plan, and His glory. He is not surprised by anything—even our sinful choices—and is very much in control.

18

Your Place in the Story

✳ *When faced with a choice, I base my decision on…*

_____

_____

✳ *When I'm making a choice, I usually talk to_____ because*

_____

_____

✳ *One choice I need to make soon is …*

✳ *I can be sure that I make a wise decision and not a hasty or prideful one by…*

_____

_____

✳ *I would say I am like (or not like) King Ahasuerus because …*

_____

_____

✳ *I would say I am like (or not like) Queen Vashti because…*

_____

_____

✳ *King Ahasuerus made some choices based on his own pride and ego, and it got him into trouble. I got in trouble for doing the same thing when I…*

_____

_____

CHAPTER 2

It Was Just an Ordinary Day . . .

MY HIGH SCHOOL WAS AN "OPEN CAMPUS," WHICH MEANT THAT STUDENTS COULD LEAVE SCHOOL FOR LUNCH. TRANSLATION: NO CAFETERIA FOOD! ONE DAY, A FRIEND AND I DECIDED TO GO TO OUT TO EAT. WE HAD THE STEREO CRANKED UP AND THE WINDOWS DOWN, ENJOYING A BEAUTIFUL FALL DAY AND THIRTY MINUTES AWAY FROM TEACHERS AND HOMEWORK.

I was driving my four-door hand-me-down car, and we were talking about the weekend homecoming game when—WHAM!—out of nowhere, we were blindsided by a monstrous work truck that careened into the back of my car, sending my side of the car into a telephone pole. I hadn't seen him turning across the lanes, and he hadn't seen me going through the intersection. (It was his fault, by the way!) Luckily, I suffered only bumps and bruises and a few shards of glass in my hair. My friend was OK too. My day had started out so calmly. It ended quite differently.

That day I learned that life is surprising. You never know what a single moment will bring. For some, the surprises are small. A minor car wreck. A pop quiz. A new crush. A change in work schedules. Some days, though, bring major, unexpected changes. Divorce. Death. Illness. Breakups. And sometimes those unexpected events can change your life, as today's Bible study will show us.

Quiz:
Do You Like Surprises?

Some people like surprises. Other people prefer to know what's on the horizon. So which are you? Take this quiz to find out.

1. When it comes to planning your future wedding, you:
   a. Have already decided on colors, bridesmaids, and style of dress.
   b. Have some general ideas in mind.
   c. Don't really think about it much and will decide later.

2. When making plans for the weekend, you decide:
   a. days in advance
   b. hours in advance
   c. weeks in advance

3. When you have a project at school, you:
   a. start working on it days before it's due
   b. start working on it when it's assigned
   c. start working on it the night before it's due

4. For a date, you would rather:
   a. plan the date yourself
   b. let him make all the plans
   c. plan the date together

5. Others would describe you as:
   a. completely spontaneous
   b. organized
   c. go with the flow

6. When a problem comes up, your first reaction is:
   a. Brief panic; then you calm down
   b. Major panic!
   c. No worries. It'll work out.

7. You prefer:
   a. lots of variety all the time
   b. a little routine but not a rut
   c. things to be in a routine

8. To keep up with your schoolwork, you use a calendar:
   a. all the time
   b. some of the time
   c. what's a calendar?

Look back over your answers and total
your score based on the chart below.

1. a=1, b=2, c=3	5. a=3, b=1, c=2
2. a=2, b=3, c=1	6. a=2, b=1, c=3
3. a=2, b=1, c=3	7. a=3, b=2, c=1
4. a=1, b=3, c=2	8. a=1, b=2, c=3

8-13 points—Miss Planner
You like to know what the next day will bring, and you prefer not to be surprised. You hate pop quizzes and unexpected changes. Planning is good, but remember that life doesn't always go as planned. Don't worry, though. God is still in control even if you are not!

14-18 points—Miss Middle Ground
You are a good combination of structure and flexibility. You like to have a plan, but you're not thrown into a tizzy if everything goes nuts. You have a good perspective of what's important. You don't miss out on the present by being too preoccupied with the future.

19-24—Miss Spontaneous
You love variety and the unexpected. Surprise parties make you happy! Keep in mind, though, that other people may not be as comfortable with change. Don't forget, sometimes having a plan is a good thing.

Meet Esther

In this chapter, you'll discover that Esther was an easy-going girl. She rolled with the punches. Wasn't shaken by the surprises life threw at her. When faced with a highly unusual situation, she responded with wisdom and grace, and the results were literally life-changing.

Mordecai:
MAWR
duh kigh

Remember how King Ahasuerus lost his wife the queen? If you need to refresh your memory, go back and read the first chapter of Esther. King Ahasuerus banished his wife Vashti because she refused to be paraded around like a piece of property in front of her husband's friends. But having kicked the queen out of the palace, he was presented with a new problem: he was now without a queen. His trusty advisors devised a solution. They thought he should have his choice of all of the beautiful women in the kingdom. That's where our story picks up.

Hegai:
HEE gigh

Read Esther 2:5-9.
✳ *Write down the characters introduced in these verses, along with a short description of each of them.*

✳ *What do you know about Esther from these verses?*

✳ *What was Esther doing before she was taken to Susa with the other girls?*

✳ *What did Hegai think of Esther? How is his opinion of Esther evident?*

✳ *If you were in Esther's shoes, how might you be feeling? Circle all the things (to the right) that you may have felt if you were in her situation.*

SAD
CONFIDENT
UNWORTHY
CONFUSED AFRAID
APATHETIC
PROUD INSECURE
HUMBLE HAPPY RESENTFUL
HONORED OVERWHELMED
EXCITED
PANICKED
PEACEFUL

Finally, We Meet Her

The curtain rises for this second act, and the main character steps onto the stage. Strangely, there is no fanfare for her. No applause, whistles, or standing ovations. No one even knows who she is. Until this point, she is merely an orphan girl adopted by her cousin because her parents are dead. She is living out her life in a foreign country, far from her homeland. Her name, though, tells us something about her. It means, "star." And she will be the star of the show later on in the story. But for now, she is one among many who are vying for the attention of one king.

Hadassah:
Hebrew name meaning "myrtle" (a tree)

Esther:
Persian name meaning "star"

Exile
In the Old Testament, when one country invaded another country and took it over, the conquering country would send people from the defeated country to the conquering country to live as foreign residents. This would keep the defeated country from organizing and mounting a defense against the conquering country. In our case, Mordecai's great-grandfather was taken back to Persia from Jerusalem when Israel was conquered in 596 B.C.

Taken, not Asked

Notice something important in verse 8. It says, "Esther was also taken to the palace." Her going was not an option. She didn't get to decide whether or not she would be included in this contest. She was herded like cattle along with all of the other women. Can you imagine being in that crowd? On the other hand, can you imagine being one of those who was NOT chosen? Not considered pretty enough to meet the king. Not tall enough or short enough. Not the right weight or body shape. Sounds an awful lot like the culture we live in today. Only the most beautiful are considered worthy. If this competition took place today, only those with perfect teeth or beautiful hair or a gorgeous body would be up for queen.

✳ *Have you ever been left out and excluded? How did you feel?*

_____

_____

_____

Eunuch:
A man who is impotent because he lacks functioning sexual organs. A male may be impotent from birth or may have been castrated. In Old Testament times, only eunuchs were allowed to care for a king's harem (for obvious reasons).

Earning Respect

Check out verse 9 again. Esther "pleased him [the eunuch Hegai] and gained his favor." Think about that one for a minute. He's a eunuch. He's missing the sexual organs that would cause him to be attracted merely to Esther's outward appearance. His thoughts toward Esther are not sexual. Something else about Esther must have impressed him—not just her good looks. He saw something in her that would appeal to the king.

✳ *What do you think Hegai saw in Esther that appealed to him and would appeal to the king?*

_____

_____

A Little History

There's one thing we know about Esther that most of the characters in the story don't know. And it will be a crucial bit of knowledge later.

Read Esther 2:5,10-11.

✳ *What key fact about Esther is hidden from outsiders?*

_____

_____

_____

✳ *Why do you think Mordecai didn't want her to tell others about her religious background?*

_____

_____

_____

✳ *How do you think you'd react to that order if you'd been Esther? Explain.*

_____

_____

_____

For some reason, Mordecai instructed Esther to keep her Jewish heritage a secret. Perhaps he knew she would have no chance to be selected as queen if people knew she was a Jew. Maybe he knew the others in the king's quarters would treat her unfairly. No one knows. But we do know that he had earned Esther's respect. She trusted him. He was more than a cousin. He was a father to her. And as such, she obeyed. Don't forget this little tidbit about her being a Jew. Tuck it away in the back of your mind. It's very important to the plot!

Esther's Big Day

Pick back up with the main plot. Esther had been taken into the king's royal court along with lots of other women for a competition like nothing you've ever seen. Think of this contest as "The Bachelor Extreme."

The greatest part of each day, each year, each lifetime is made up of small, seemingly insignificant moments.

(Barbara Coloroso)

Read Esther 2:12-14.

✳ *What was the process for each woman? What happened before, during, and after her appearance before the king?*

_____

_____

_____

Myrrh:
An expensive and aromatic gum taken from a shrub and turned into an oil substance that could be massaged into the skin.

✳ *What did the women focus on? What did they not focus on?*

_____

_____

_____

✳ *Where did the women go if not chosen as the king's new queen?*

_____

_____

✳ *How do you think these women felt? How would you have felt?*

_____

_____

_____

Twelve months of beauty treatments. Talk about the spa treatment! For a full year, these women underwent the equivalent of facial scrubs, body peels, and massages with expensive oils and perfumes. It may have seemed like a grand party, but stop and think for a minute. Can you imagine being taken from your home, separated from your family and friends, and living with a bunch of other women? Some scholars think there could have been as many as 400 women gathered for this contest! 400! Can you imagine the catfights? The bickering? The gossip? The hormones run amuck? While it may seem like these women were living in luxury, they paid a high price for their mud baths.

A Night in the Palace

When her name was called, each woman would go to the palace at
night to meet the king. She could take with her anything she wanted in
order to make an impression. Special clothes. Jewelry. Gifts. Whatever.
It would need to be unique in order for a girl to stand out among 400
women. She would then spend the night with the king and return to a
second harem in the morning.

I know you're asking yourself, does "spend the night" mean what
I think it means? Yep. You're right. Each of these virgins lost their
virginity because a king lost his temper and wanted a new queen. (Add
these girls to the list of people affected by the king's anger and rash
decisions. And then add their parents, friends, and future spouses to
the list.) Then, to make matters worse, if the woman was not chosen,
she was taken to live in a second harem of women, where she would live
out her days like a widow—never to marry again, never to see the king
again unless he asked her to return. She did not go home to her family.
She did not go back to her life as she had known it. No wedding bells
would ever be on the horizon. She could have everything she wanted,
but she was a virtual prisoner of the king.

*Think about Esther's situation for a moment. How would you act if you faced
this situation?*

And the Winner Is . . .

Finally, the time had come for Esther to meet the king. You've probably
been nervous before, but can you imagine the case of butterflies that
was settling into Esther's stomach?

Read Esther 2:15-18.

✳ *What did Esther bring with her to meet the king?*

_____

_____

✳ *Why do you think she relied on Hegai?*

_____

_____

✳ *What does this little action tell you about Esther's character?*

_____

_____

_____

✳ *Why do you think Esther won the approval of everyone who saw her, including the king?*

_____

_____

_____

I have never had clarity. What I have always had is trust.

(Mother Teresa)

Put yourself in Esther's glass slippers for a minute. If you were Esther, what would be going through your mind? What would be going on in your heart? In the space provided, write a diary entry about all that has happened to you up to this point and tell your diary everything you are feeling.

DEAR DIARY...

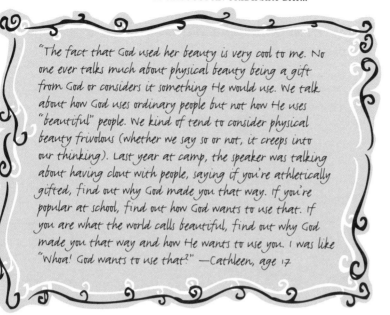

"The fact that God used her beauty is very cool to me. No one ever talks much about physical beauty being a gift from God or considers it something He would use. We talk about how God uses ordinary people but not how He uses "beautiful" people. We kind of tend to consider physical beauty frivolous (whether we say so or not, it creeps into our thinking). Last year at camp, the speaker was talking about having clout with people, saying if you're athletically gifted, find out why God made you that way. If you're popular at school, find out how God wants to use that. If you are what the world calls beautiful, find out why God made you that way and how He wants to use you. I was like "Whoa! God wants to use that?" —Cathleen, age 17

We don't know why King Ahasuerus chose Esther. But you can bet that something about her was different. Something stood out. Maybe it was wisdom. She certainly demonstrated that by taking with her only what Hegai (who would know the king's likes and dislikes) suggested that she take for her one night with the king. Maybe it was her ability to adjust to changing situations. She showed that trait as she participated in this massive beauty pageant. And maybe, just maybe, he saw her trust in God. She would definitely need to trust that God was in the midst of the situation and was working things out. Otherwise, she would be totally overwhelmed, confused, and afraid. Any girl would be. But Esther didn't panic. She let events unfold, even if she didn't understand what they meant for her life. Only later would she understand all the reasons God had placed her in such an unusual situation.

Esther's example is a good one for us to follow. Life happens. Sometimes we have no control over how it unfolds. Death strikes. Divorce devastates. Your dad's job moves you to a new state. You start dating. Your family faces financial struggles. Friendships come and go. We can only see the scenes of our lives as they unfold. We are in the middle of a story that is still being told. But it's good to know that God knows the end of our lives from the beginning. He is already there, so we can trust Him.

31

The Plot Thickens

To close this chapter, we need to look at a few more verses. While this is not a pivotal part of the story right now, you don't want to miss out on major piece of the plot. This little subplot will be a BIG deal later. So read it now...

Read Esther 2:19-23.

✴ *Fill in the chart of characters to tell their roles in this part of the story. One is supplied for you:*

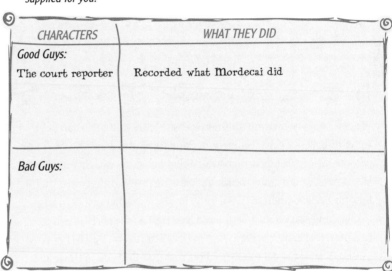

CHARACTERS	WHAT THEY DID
Good Guys: The court reporter	Recorded what Mordecai did
Bad Guys:	

In a nutshell, two eunuchs got mad at the king, and instead of working out at the gym to release their aggression, they decided to plot an assassination. Not a good plan. Mordecai overheard them and told Esther, who told the king. These two ended up dead and this whole event was written down in the court records. (Remember that!)

Your Place in the Story

* Have you ever faced a time in your life when things took an unexpected turn and nothing would ever be the same? When you knew your life would never be like it had been before? Journal about it.

* How do you typically respond when something unexpected happens?

* What character traits of Esther that you saw in this chapter do you exhibit in your own life? How?

* What character traits of Esther that you saw in this chapter do you most need to develop? Explain.

* Why is it sometimes hard for you to trust God when the unexpected happens?

* Who in your life is a great example of trusting God when the unexpected happens? Why?

CHAPTER 3

Standing Alone

I HATED JUNIOR HIGH AND HIGH SCHOOL. I HATED FEELING INSECURE AND UNSURE OF MYSELF. I HATED THAT THE SCHOOL WAS DIVIDED INTO GROUPS. THE NERDS. THE POPULAR KIDS. THE DRUGGIES. THE EARLY BLOOMERS. THE LATE BLOOMERS. AND THE NOBODIES. I WAS A NOBODY. I DIDN'T REALLY FIT INTO ANY CATEGORY.

I wasn't particularly pretty. I wasn't a basketball star or a cheerleader. I was a nameless face in the crowd and desperately wanted to be in the popular crowd. But since I wasn't rich and didn't have great looks, that dream was never going to come true. So I did what most girls my age did—I gossiped about the popular kids. Trash-talked them every chance I got. It made me feel better. I'm embarrassed to admit it now.

One particular day, I was trashing a girl named Kelly. She was on the basketball team. She was a cheerleader. And she lived in the new subdivision where all the rich kids lived. Standing at my locker one day, I made a comment to my best friend about some juicy bit of gossip I had heard (or even made up—I don't remember which). One of Kelly's friends happened to be standing at a nearby locker and heard me trashing Kelly. She walked right up to me and said: "No, that's not true. Stop saying that." I was stunned. Mortified. Shocked. And silenced.

Looking back on what Kelly's friend did, I am amazed at her willing-ness to speak up for a friend, especially in junior high when all you want to do is fit in. She took a chance and took a stand. Kelly's friend showed some real courage that day.

How about you? Are you willing to take a stand for what you believe? Take the quiz on the next page to find out.

Quiz
Will You Stand?

1. When a classmate says something negative about Christianity, you:
   a. don't say anything
   b. speak if spoken to
   c. burst out with a ready defense

2. Your friend wants you to pass on a text message about something embarrassing that happened to a girl you know. You:
   a. send it after you edit the most embarrassing parts
   b. send it along, no questions asked.
   c. don't send it. Next time, it could be you!

3. When the subject of creation versus evolution comes up in your science class, you:
   a. keep quiet
   b. write a paper on why the evolution theory is faulty
   c. give your opinion if asked

4. You are sitting in a waiting room with no empty seats. An elderly lady walks in and needs a place to sit. You:
   a. take quick action to give up your seat
   b. keep your seat
   c. give up your seat if no one else will

5. Your crush finally asks you out. Later, he wants the two of you to go to his house alone. You:
   a. get nervous and suggest going to a friend's house instead
   b. tell him you don't think it's a good idea.
   c. go ahead

6. You see a bunch of seniors pick on a geeky freshman. You:
   a. keep your mouth shut and keep walking
   b. go tell a teacher
   c. walk into the group and stop the harassment

7. Your friends want to see the latest R-rated flick. You:
   a. suggest a PG-13 movie instead.
   b. don't argue. Majority rules.
   c. tell them no. Your parents would freak!

8. You hear an off-color joke about people of another nationality. You:
   a. walk away
   b. say something to the joke-teller
   c. keep quiet

9. Your health teacher tells the class that homosexuality is a healthy type of sexual expression. You:
   a. keep quiet
   b. write a letter of protest
   c. tell your student minister

10. A bunch of girls are gossiping about the new girl in school. You:
    a. change the subject
    b. keep quiet
    c. make friends with the girl

11. You act differently around your non-Christian friends:
    a. always
    b. sometimes
    c. never

How did you do on the quiz? There are no right or wrong answers to some of the questions. The quiz was designed just to help you start thinking about the issues that matter to you, things you'd be willing to take a stand for. Standing up against wrong is not easy. In fact, it can make us downright uncomfortable. In today's lesson, we'll see one man's example of standing firm even when the pressure was almost unbearable.

A Little Review

✳ *How much do you remember about a guy called Mordecai? In the space provided, jot down everything you can recall.*

In today's story, Esther actually steps off stage and another plotline emerges. It involves Mordecai and a man named Haman.

Read Esther 3:1-6.

✳ *What was Haman's ethnic background (v. 1)? What was Mordecai's (v. 4)?*

✳ *Whom did King Ahasuerus honor? How was he honored?*

✳ *Now think back to the last chapter. Who uncovered the plot to assassinate the king? How did the king honor him?*

✳ *Who refused to honor Haman? Why do you think he refused?*

✳ *How did the other people respond to Mordecai's actions? Why do you think they behaved that way?*

✳ *How did Haman respond to Mordecai's actions? Whom was he planning to kill?*

New Character in the Drama

Another character enters the spotlight. When Haman steps out on stage, you instantly know that he is not a man who struggles with his self-esteem. He doesn't need to see a counselor about his insecurity issues. Haman has a grande-sized ego, fueled by the king who commanded that people bow and pay homage to Haman. And everyone obeys—everyone except Mordecai. The Bible does not tell us specifically why Mordecai doesn't bow down to Haman, but it does give us a couple of clues. Remember that Mordecai and Esther are Jews. Haman, on the other hand, is an Agagite. While that may not seem like a big deal to you and me, it was VERY significant in Esther's day. An Agagite was a descendant of Agag, an Amalekite king who fought against the Jews earlier in their history. To make a very long and complicated story

Haman:
HAY muhn

39

short, Haman's ancestors hated Mordecai's ancestors. And the feeling was mutual. So Mordecai bowing to Haman? Not gonna happen. Ever.

The second clue about why Mordecai refused to bow is also connected to his being Jewish. Remember that the Jews refused to bow to anyone or anything besides Jehovah, the one true God. (Remember the Ten Commandments?) For Mordecai to bow to another god or another man would be considered idolatry, which was a grave sin in the eyes of God. So Mordecai bowing to Haman? Again, not gonna happen. Ever.

To make matters worse, King Ahasuerus promoted Haman and failed to honor Mordecai for foiling an assassination plot. In fact, up to this point, the king had done nothing to thank Mordecai. Instead, Mordecai must watch an enemy be promoted instead. That must have been difficult for Mordecai to accept. I bet you've felt the same way. When a classmate cheats and gets an A. Or when that mean girl gets the guy and you're left alone at homecoming. It's tough to watch.

Mordecai's motives may be a little mixed between his devotion to God and his own pride, but you have to give him credit for standing firm in his convictions. Even though his disobedience was in direct violation to the king's orders, he wouldn't budge. Everyone around him was bowing to Haman, but he wouldn't. The rest of the royal staff bowed. They even asked him why he wasn't going along with the orders: "Everyone else is doing it. Why aren't you?" Day after day the staff warned him. But Mordecai stood firm, refusing to go along with the group. He refused to take part in something that he knew in his heart was wrong.

Hatred corrodes the vessel in which it is stored.

(Chinese proverb)

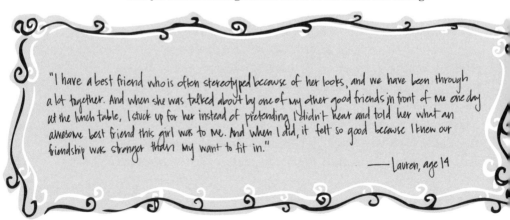

"I have a best friend who is often stereotyped because of her looks, and we have been through a lot together. And when she was talked about by one of my other good friends in front of me one day at the lunch table, I stuck up for her instead of pretending I didn't hear and told her what an awesome best friend this girl was to me. And when I did, it felt so good because I knew our friendship was stronger than my want to fit in."

—Lauren, age 14

Your Turn

✳ *Do you ever feel like Mordecai? Have you ever felt pressure to do something you knew in your heart was wrong? Do you ever struggle with worrying what will happen if you don't do what someone else wants? In the boxes below are several situations that you probably face or might face in the future. Write down in each of the boxes what you fear might happen if you don't give into that pressure.*

Cheating

Gossiping

Oral sex

Lying to parents

Bullying

Wearing immodest clothes

Materialism

Other

It's tough being in those situations. It's hard to feel like you are the oddball. It's uncomfortable knowing that you are choosing the toughest path. Here's an important thing to keep in mind: nothing is worth sacrificing what you believe in. Your character is worth more than what others think. While it may feel uncomfortable to go against popular opinion, it's even more gut-wrenching to go against everything you believe.

Feeling like Haman

It's easy to root for Mordecai because you can understand what he's going through, what he must be feeling. It's easy to root against Haman. But before you come down on Haman too much, answer one difficult question: Have you ever wished bad things for someone? Hoped the prom queen would get embarrassed? Wanted the school jock to get caught cheating? Wished your sister or brother would get into trouble? Hoped your chemistry teacher would come down with a nasty virus? Maybe there's a little bit of Haman in all of us, that sinful part of us that allows our own ego and pride to get the best of us. That sinful side that hides at church but is there anyway. I'm not saying that Haman's actions are justified or acceptable in any way. I'm just saying that we're a lot more like Haman than we would want to admit.

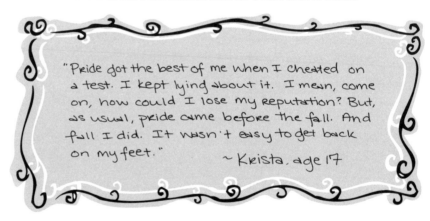

"Pride got the best of me when I cheated on a test. I kept lying about it. I mean, come on, how could I lose my reputation? But, as usual, pride came before the fall. And fall I did. It wasn't easy to get back on my feet."

~ Krista, age 17

Haman's Nasty Plan

If you disliked Haman to begin with, you're really going to dislike him as he shows why he earned the title of villain in the story. He earns it with his nasty plan and deceptive maneuvering. Read Esther 3:7-11 to see what happens. Then complete the activity on the next page.

✳ *Act as if you are a newspaper reporter covering the events told in these verses. Answer the basic questions: who, what, when, where, why, and how. Write your newspaper story in the space provided.*

Yep. Haman was a nasty little schemer. He lied to the king and told him that a group of people (the Jews) had infiltrated the Persian culture. These rebels were defying the king's laws (How dare they!) and needed to be exterminated for the king's best interest. (Oh, please…Haman had his best interests at heart!) Haman even offered to fund the annihilation plan. It was a bribe of massive proportions. He would deposit 375 tons of silver into the royal treasury. Can you guess where he would get that kind of money? Yep! He would take the money belonging to the Jews he would kill. Not only would he kill innocent people, but he would take their money as well.

MO' MONEY
Haman's bribe of silver amounted to between one-half to two-thirds of the annual revenue of the empire!

At this point in the story, you begin to question the leadership skills of King Ahasuerus. He hasn't exactly been the sharpest crayon in the box. In his pride and arrogance, he banned his first queen. Then, he promoted a man of VERY questionable character, Haman, to be the prime minister of his country and failed to honor a man who saved his life. Then he allowed Haman to talk him into destroying a whole nation of people (including the man who had saved his life) without asking any questions. He even gave Haman his signet ring as a sign of approval and money to fund the whole operation. This king didn't demonstrate an ounce of wisdom or strength of character. But that will change, thankfully. (Don't worry, I won't spoil it for you!)

LOTS:
("pur" in Hebrew) Objects of unknown shape and material used to determine an outcome. When a person cast lots, he was trying to make a decision and believed that God (or gods, in the case of non-Jews) influenced the way the lots fell, thus showing the person what to choose. In this story, Haman used lots to decide on a date to annihilate the Jews.

Chaos in the Kingdom

What the king ordered to be carried out would affect thousands, if not millions, of innocent people who had nothing to do with the conflict between Haman and Mordecai. They were casualties of war, caught in the crossfire between two people, two egos, and two systems of belief. Find out how extensive Haman's plan was.

Read Esther 3:12-15.

✳ *What did the letters tell the officials to do in every province in the kingdom?*

✳ *On what day were the orders written? When would they be carried out? (The answer to this may be a little confusing. Don't worry. Just jot it down anyway.)*

✳ *At the end of this chapter, what were King Ahasuerus and Haman doing?*

✳ *What was the mood of the people in Susa?*

SIGNET RING: A signet ring had a seal crafted upon it. This seal authenticated a document, much like a signature would today. Often, a king would melt wax on top of a document, sealing the document. Then, while the wax was still hot, the king would stamp his ring into the wax, leaving the seal impression behind. It was a symbol of authority and power.

Do not miss the power of this edict. It was given by the king's authority. It could never be revoked. Every man, woman, and child of Jewish heritage was destined for death. No wonder the city of Susa was thrown into such massive confusion. No doubt the people were wondering why such a law was put into place. More than likely, most Persians and Jews got along just fine. They probably lived next door to each other. Borrowed flour and eggs from each other. Their kids probably played soccer together (well, maybe not, but you get the point). More than likely, they bartered in business dealings. And now, an edict had been handed down that would destroy every Jew. No wonder the people were in a total state of shock and confusion! And yet, clueless to the concerns of his people, King Ahasuerus kicked back and had a drink with Haman.

Did you see when the notice was sent out? Did you notice when the Jews would be killed? In modern terms, the death decree was sent out in the first month of the year. But the edict to kill the Jews would not be carried out until the twelfth month of the year. An entire year of waiting, watching, listening. An entire year to wonder how death would come. An entire year to plead with God to spare the lives of loved ones. An entire year to worry, wonder, and wait. And like a great play, this scene ends at this cliffhanger, leaving you to wonder what will happen. This is Haman's moment of glory. Everything is going his way.

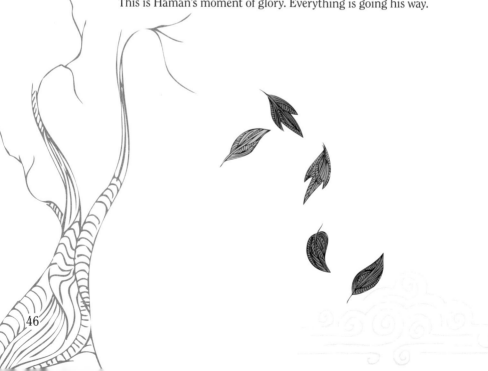

Your Place in the Story

✳ Sometimes I am like Haman when I...

_____

_____

✳ When a difficult situation comes my way, I typically feel...

_____

_____

_____

✳ One person I really admire for standing up for her beliefs is _____because...

_____

_____

_____

✳ I am confused why God would allow...

_____

_____

_____

✳ I stood up for what I believed when I...

_____

_____

_____

✳ As a result of standing up for my beliefs...

_____

_____

✳ Like Mordecai, I need to stand up for my beliefs in this area:

_____

_____

✳ I will do this by taking the following actions:

_____

_____

CHAPTER 4

A Place in the Plan

NOT TOO LONG AGO, I WENT WITH SOME FRIENDS TO A MOVIE, A REAL ADVENTURE FLICK WITH CHASE SCENES AND BAD GUYS AND PLOT TWISTS AND THINGS THAT BLEW UP IN A BIG FIREBALL.

We filed into the theater with popcorn in one hand and soda in the other. We were the first ones there (I hate to miss the previews so I always go early!), so we got the prime seats—center stage, halfway up, eye-level to the main part of the screen. After what seemed like forever, the lights dimmed, the commercials played, and the trailers hooked me into future releases. Then the movie started.

I was engrossed, literally sitting on the edge of my seat. My heart rate escalated. My nerves were frayed. (I tend to become very involved in movies. In fact, I have to wear my glasses instead of contacts because I forget to blink, causing my contacts to become fused to my eyeballs.) And at the peak of the conflict, the unthinkable happened. The fire alarms went off! Lights flashing. Horns blaring. Ushers running around with orange vests and flashlights. Everyone in the theater was evacuated. We were forced outside into the night air (which was quite cold, by the way) to contemplate the impending doom of our hero. Everyone talked about how they thought the story would end (nobody was right!). Everybody was anxious and frustrated. We all wanted back inside and back to our story. Back to our hero's plight. Back to the drama. We'd been left hanging!

The Conflict Surges

In the last chapter, the story left us hanging. Mordecai (Esther's cousin) refused to bow down to Haman. An enraged and arrogant Haman plotted against Mordecai (a Jew) by convincing and bribing the king to sign an edict to have all the Jews in Persia annihilated. Mordecai was in trouble, and so were all the other Jews. The picture looks pretty bleak. A king's orders could not be ignored. Like a great story, the conflict is escalating to a dramatic conclusion.

Sackcloth: Rough clothing worn as a sign of grief for the dead or as a symbol of sorrow over a disaster. Also worn as a sign of repentance. Sackcloth was made of goat or camel hair.

Read Esther 4:1-3.

✳ *How did Mordecai respond to the edict to have the Jews killed and their belongings plundered?*

✳ *What was the response of other Jews in Susa?*

✳ *What are some ways you have seen people deal with their grief? How have you dealt with loss? Check all that apply to you and to other people you know. Then circle the ones you think would be most helpful for you:*

☐ *cried*   ☐ *wore black*   ☐ *couldn't eat*

☐ *journaled*   ☐ *slept a lot*   ☐ *read the Bible*

☐ *hit something*   ☐ *planted a tree*   ☐ *ate a lot*

☐ *wrote poetry*   ☐ *listened to music*   ☐ *couldn't sleep*

☐ *prayed*   ☐ *used drugs*   ☐ *talked*

☐ *yelled at God*   ☐ *got angry*   ☐ *drank*

☐ *self-injured*   ☐ *watched sad movies*   ☐ *curled up under a blanket*

51

Getting Some Attention

When word of the annihilation reached Mordecai, he put on sackcloth and ashes. Seems pretty odd to you and me. You don't see many people walking through the mall wearing a skirt made of goat hair and covered from head to toe in ashes. But in Esther's day, it showed sorrow or grief, much like wearing black to a funeral today.

Scripture doesn't tell us why Mordecai wore the sackcloth and ashes. Obviously, he knew his life and the lives of thousands of others had been threatened by an edict from the king. Things didn't look good for the Jewish people. But what if there were other reasons for Mordecai's unusual choice in clothes? Perhaps he knew that his encounter with Haman (remember, Mordecai refused to bow to him) had sparked this insane chain of events. And perhaps he wanted to act in a way that would get Esther's attention. Whatever his motives, Mordecai's behavior caught the attention of others.

✳ *Read Esther 4:4-8. Put into order the events that took place in these verses.*

_____ *Mordecai (through Hathach) urged Esther to go into the king's presence to plead for the Jewish people.*

_____ *Esther sent clothes for Mordecai to wear instead of sackcloth.*

_____ *Mordecai told Hathach about the plot to destroy the Jews.*

_____ *Esther summoned Hathach to find out what was bothering Mordecai.*

_____ *Esther's maids and eunuchs told her about Mordecai's behavior.*

✳ *Why do you think people told Esther about Mordecai's behavior?*

_____

_____

✳ *Why do you think Esther sent Mordecai clothes to wear instead of sackcloth?*

_____

_____

✻ Why do you think Mordecai presented Esther all of the evidence (the exact
   amount of the bribe, the copy of the edict, etc.) of the annihilation plan?

✻ What was Mordecai's plea to Esther?

The Story Reaches Esther

Esther's maids and eunuchs told her about Mordecai. The writer
doesn't tell us why they delivered the message. Perhaps they kept
her up on the palace rumors. Perhaps she had told them to keep her
informed on any issues that faced the nation. Or perhaps, somehow,
they knew she was related to Mordecai. We do know their report set
into motion a flurry of events. First Esther tried to calm Mordecai
down, sending him a different set of clothes to wear. When Mordecai
refused the clothes, she sent a eunuch named Hathach to find out why
Mordecai flipped out.

Hathach:
HAY thak

Like a skilled lawyer laying out his case before a jury, Mordecai relayed
everything that happened. The edict. The money promised. Possibly
even the confrontation between him and Haman that started it all. And
in a closing argument, Mordecai pleaded with his adopted daughter to
go talk to the king. The evidence was overwhelming. The Jews were
headed for the firing squad. Esther had to help her people.

Talk about a great movie plot. Our heroine Esther found out that her
nation, the Jews, had been sentenced to death by her own husband!
And until this point, she had no idea what was going on! I can't
imagine what went through her mind. She was an orphan living in the
king's palace. And she'd just been told that the Jewish people (including
her beloved cousin Mordecai) were marked for death. And yet, Mordecai's challenge to go speak to the king seemed a bit overwhelming.

✳ *Read Esther 4:9-17. Picture this as a conversation between two friends over a cup of coffee. Use the space below to summarize the dialogue between Esther and Mordecai.*

Esther: (verses 11-12)

_____

_____

Mordecai: (verses 12-14)

_____

Esther: (verses 15-16)

_____

Mordecai: (verse 17)

_____

Before you label Esther as a coward, put yourself in her shoes. Remember how she became queen? The former queen had been banished for defying the king. And now, Mordecai wanted her to defy the king's laws. It could mean instant death. No wonder Esther was a little hesitant. Besides, it'd been a while since she had seen the king. What if he didn't like her anymore? What if he got angry at her for breaking protocol? But just because Esther was a little hesitant didn't mean she lacked courage. She had questions. Doubts. Concerns. And fear. Keep in mind, though, that courage is not the absence of fear.

The Role of a Lifetime

Mordecai's response to Esther is one of the most famous in Scripture. It would make a great trailer for the movie. He said in essence, "Don't think that your own life will be spared. Your head may be on the chopping block too. God will deliver the Jewish people with or without you, but you and your family will die if you do nothing. And who knows? Maybe God made you Queen of Persia for such a time as this."

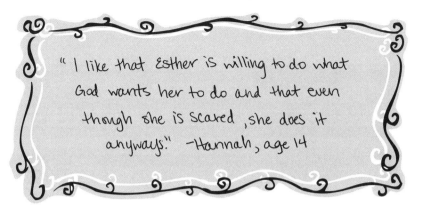

" I like that Esther is willing to do what God wants her to do and that even though she is scared, she does it anyways." —Hannah, age 14

It's hard to argue with Mordecai. He let his words fly all over Esther. No excuses. No easy way out. No giving into the fear. It's as if he said, "Step it up, Esther. It's time for you to walk on stage. It's time for you to play the real-life role of a lifetime. Maybe God has made you queen for this critical moment. Don't miss it." Mordecai must have suspected God had been at work, placing Esther at the right place and time to play a critical role in the history of the Jews. And Esther had a choice to make.

YOUR TURN:

✴ Who are the Mordecais in your life—the people who have confronted you and not let you make excuses? How have they shaped your life?

_____

_____

_____

Read Esther 4:15-17 again.

✴ What was Esther's response to Mordecai? What was her plan?

_____

_____

✴ Why do you think Esther wanted the Jews to fast and pray?

_____

_____

_____

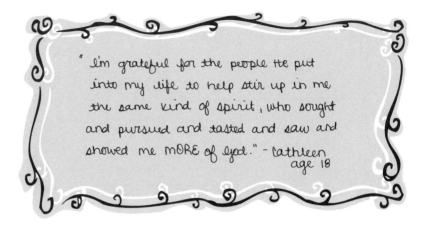

"I'm grateful for the people He put into my life to help stir up in me the same kind of spirit, who sought and pursued and tasted and saw and showed me MORE of God." - Cathleen age 18

Fasting:
To go without food or drink for a period of time. Sometimes done as a group or by individuals. Sometimes done as a demonstration of repentance or grief. Also done in order to focus one's attention more clearly on God. Usually done in conjunction with a concentrated time of prayer. Today, people fast from a variety of things: a certain food, coffee, music, TV, a relationship, etc. The time usually spent with these things (such as an hour of television) is devoted to focused time with God.

✳ *What does verse 16 tell us about Esther's attitude?*

Mordecai's pep talk did the trick. Esther came up with a plan. She told Mordecai to gather all of the Jews to fast for her for three days. And since fasting normally involved prayer, she was asking the entire Jewish nation to intercede for her. She understood the power of prayer.

After the three days of fasting and praying, she would go talk to the king even though it was against the law. She would take a stand and help her people, regardless of the consequences. Whether she lived or died, even if she was banished like Vashti, she would go.

YOUR TURN:
✳ *Where has God placed you for a specific reason at a specific moment? Think about your own life. Use the space below to write down strategic places God has placed you to use you to honor Him.*

Your Place in the Story

✳ One time, I was really sad about_____. I worked through my grief by…

_____

_____

_____

✳ I am really afraid of _____ because…

_____

_____

_____

✳ I need to take a stand in this area in my life (circle those that apply):

AT CHURCH WITH MY BOYFRIEND WITH A FRIEND

ON THE TEAM AT WORK ONLINE AT SCHOOL

AT HOME IN THE CAFETERIA

✳ I need to take a stand by:

_____

_____

_____

✳ A person I admire for his/her courage is _____ because…

_____

_____

_____

CHAPTER 5

Behind the Scenes

I AM DEATHLY AFRAID OF HEIGHTS. ACTUALLY, I AM NOT AFRAID OF HEIGHTS; I AM ONLY AFRAID OF PLUNGING TO MY DEATH AFTER FALLING FROM GREAT HEIGHTS.

When I was a little girl, I used to have a recurring nightmare that I was on a roller coaster, and its tracks ran out as it rounded a loop. Just when I would ride upside down in the loop, the track would disappear, and I would plunge down to the depths below. (I always woke up before I hit the ground—weird, huh?)

Last summer, I decided to conquer (or at least tame) my fear of heights. I decided to go parasailing. I was in Florida on vacation and saw tons of people flying up in the air strapped to a parachute-looking thingy tethered to a boat. It looked like so much fun. The people on the brochures were all smiling. The rational side of me said, "Look, you're connected to the earth (or at least a boat) with a big, shiny cord. Nothing could happen. You can't let fear rob you of trying something new. You'll miss out if you don't try it." So in a more rational moment of the day, I called and made reservations. No problem.

No problem, that is, until I got to the boat the next day. Then, the not-so-logical part of me started talking. "What if the cord breaks? What if a huge gust of wind comes and lifts me up into the outer stratosphere? What if someone has rigged the chute to fail so the company will go out of business? (I know, I watch too much TV.) What if a big yacht speeds by, creating a wake that capsizes the boat? Then what?

After swallowing hard and going to the bathroom about a gazillion times (nerves), I went into the office and signed a waiver stating that I would not sue the company if I met my impending doom while in their care. Then I stepped onto the boat, and we took off. I prayed.

And prayed. And tried to think happy thoughts instead of scenarios that included my death. More swallowing. More needing to go to the bathroom (which was a problem since I was now out on the water). At last, it was my turn at parasailing. The deck hands strapped me in, laughing to each other as I was reassuring myself about how I wasn't going to die. I sat on the back of the boat like I was told and waited. Then, as the boat accelerated and the wind filled the parachute, I was up in the air. Gliding. I felt like I was sitting in a swing as the wind carried me higher and higher. It was one of the coolest experiences I'd ever had. The fear was gone, replaced by joy and excitement. To be honest, I didn't want to come back down to earth.

In last week's study, we learned that courage doesn't mean the absence of fear. It means doing something even when you're scared. Are you willing to be courageous?

✳ *Listed below are different activities. Rate yourself on whether you'd be willing to do each thing. A low number means there's no way you'd do it. A high number means you're all in.*

1 2 3 4 5 6 7 8 9 10   *Talk to a guy you really like (and he doesn't know you like him)*

1 2 3 4 5 6 7 8 9 10   *Go skydiving*

1 2 3 4 5 6 7 8 9 10   *Speak up in Bible study*

1 2 3 4 5 6 7 8 9 10   *Stand up for a girl being bullied*

1 2 3 4 5 6 7 8 9 10   *Give a speech at school*

1 2 3 4 5 6 7 8 9 10   *Ask your parents for help*

1 2 3 4 5 6 7 8 9 10   *Stand up for a friend who's being gossiped about*

1 2 3 4 5 6 7 8 9 10   *Talk about God*

1 2 3 4 5 6 7 8 9 10   *Go overseas for the summer*

1 2 3 4 5 6 7 8 9 10   *Say no to alcohol at a party*

1 2 3 4 5 6 7 8 9 10   *Tell a guy to stop when you've gone too far physically*

1 2 3 4 5 6 7 8 9 10   *Give a baby up for adoption instead of having an abortion*

1 2 3 4 5 6 7 8 9 10   *Try out for cheerleader or a sports team*

1 2 3 4 5 6 7 8 9 10   *Sing in front of people*

1 2 3 4 5 6 7 8 9 10   *Run for office (class president, secretary, etc.)*

1 2 3 4 5 6 7 8 9 10   *Ask a teacher for help*

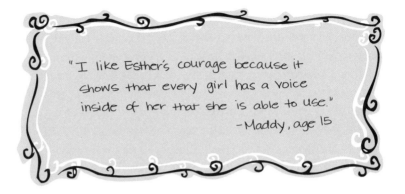

"I like Esther's courage because it shows that every girl has a voice inside of her that she is able to use."
—Maddy, age 15

Courage Under Fire

Esther demonstrated her own brand of courage as she reappeared on stage for a dramatic encounter with King Ahasuerus and his right-hand man, Haman. Our heroine Esther found herself in a difficult situation. Yet, her courage won out over her fear, and she chose to stand in the gap for her people. Esther decided to approach the king.

Read Esther 5:1-7.

* *How many days passed between the time Mordecai told Esther about the edict to kill the Jews and when Esther went before the king?*

* *She had 11 months before the sentence was to be carried out. Why do you think she went so quickly to see King Ahasuerus?*

* *Why do you think she chose not to go through the proper protocol to make a formal request to see the king?*

* *How did Esther dress? Why do you think she dressed that way?*

* *What do you think was going through Haman's mind as Esther made her unusual request?*

* *Why do you think she asked the king and Haman to come to a second banquet?*

Wow. I cannot imagine how nervous Esther must have been as she prepared to meet the king. It makes parasailing seem like flying a kite. Yet, despite her anxiety and nervousness, Esther went into the palace, disregarding protocol to speak to the king unsummoned. I picture her moments before she went before the king: trying to control her breathing, wiping her sweaty palms on the side of her dress, taking a second (or third or fourth) look in the mirror, making sure every hair was in place, swallowing hard, trying to walk confidently when her knees felt like jelly, praying all the way.

Scripture says that as soon as Ahasuerus saw Esther, she won his approval, and he extended his scepter to her. Knowing that Esther was acting out of protocol, the king asked the obvious question: What's wrong? Finally, this was her chance! She could have asked the king for help. But Esther's response was a little strange: come to a banquet I've prepared. She didn't throw herself at the king's feet and beg him to save her people. She didn't go all drama queen and cry uncontrollably. She asked for the king and Haman to come eat. Seems strange, doesn't it? And what is even more odd is that at that banquet, when the king again asked Esther what she wanted, she still didn't tell him. Instead, she requested that the king and Haman return the next day for another banquet, where she'd finally tell him what she wanted. The tension is mounting. The confrontation is coming. It's almost unbearable.

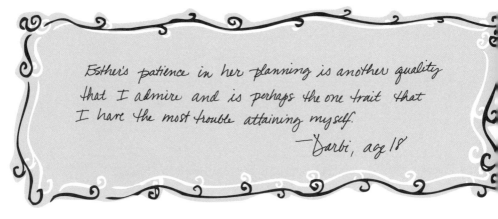

Esther's patience in her planning is another quality that I admire and is perhaps the one trait that I have the most trouble attaining myself.

—Darbi, age 18

So why this mystery? Why not just state the facts and ask for help? Why make the king wait? Why put herself at further risk? (If I were king, I'd be pretty ticked if I asked a question twice and didn't get a response.) Whatever the reason, Esther's actions showed her courage and her character. She was patient and wise, willing to watch things unfold as she waited for the right moment.

Your Turn
* Would people say you are patient? Why or why not?

_____

_____

* Would others say you are wise? Why or why not?

_____

_____

_____

Haman's Mood
Can you imagine Haman's mood? He's loaded with pride because he's the king's prime minister. Nobody was better in the kingdom (except for the king). Everybody bowed to him. And now, Queen Esther had invited him to two banquets. Not just one banquet, but two! And nobody else was invited! He must have been anxious to go home and tell his wife about his day. Too bad things didn't go quite as planned...

Read Esther 5:9-14.

✳ *What happened to Haman on the way home?*

_____

_____

_____

✳ *What was his wife's advice?*

_____

_____

_____

Hanging
In verse 14, the term hanging does not refer to being suffocated by a rope. It means something quite gruesome: being impaled on a huge pole or stake!

Poor, poor Haman. It didn't matter that he was outrageously wealthy. Forget the fact that he'd been blessed with many sons (a big deal in his day). He could care less that the king had promoted him to a position higher than any other staff. None of it mattered because of one man: Mordecai. The guy just wouldn't bow to Haman. And it enraged Haman. Made him lose perspective. Robbed his joy. Stole his peace. Haman was so undone by Mordecai that the only thing that made him feel better was the thought of Mordecai dead on the gallows. He could not even wait until the edict was carried out in eleven months. He wanted Mordecai humiliated immediately. How sad is that?

Your Turn

It's easy to look down on Haman for his outright hatred toward Mordecai. But if you're honest, you might admit that you've had your own "Mordecai," that one person who gets under your skin. You have been blessed with friends and family and possessions, but you've lost perspective. You can't enjoy any of it because you're obsessed with her. Maybe she is dating your ex. Perhaps she's prettier than you. Or possibly she started a stupid rumor about you months ago.

✳ *Who is your Mordecai?*

_____

_____

*What has she (or he) done?

_____

_____

_____

*How have you lost perspective? What have you missed out on because of your
sour attitude?

_____

_____

_____

The same God who worked in Esther's life is working in yours. Nothing in your life slips through the hands of God unnoticed.

King Ahasuerus and Mordecai

Remember what Mordecai did for the king earlier in the story? If
you can't recall, look back at Esther 2:21-23. Mordecai's time in the
limelight is finally here, much to the dismay of Haman.

Read Esther 6:1-11.

*What was wrong with the king and how did he attempt to fix this problem?

_____

_____

_____

*What did the king learn? How did he respond to this news?

_____

_____

*Who was in the court when the king learned about this? Why was he there?

_____

_____

_____

✻ What was Haman's suggestion? Why was he so lavish?

If this were a movie, then this chapter of Esther would be the comic irony. You have to laugh at Haman. The guy just can't win. He came to the palace to talk to the king about having Mordecai hanged. When he arrived, the king ushered him in to ask him how to honor a man. In his own arrogance, Haman thought the king wanted to honor him, so he came up with an amazing demonstration of favor. Royal garments. A massive stallion. A crown on his head. Paraded around the city by a high-ranking official who would shout the man's praises. Haman was pleased with his plan. And then came the zinger. The king commanded him to go and do it all for Mordecai!

This chapter is an amazing demonstration of a truth introduced earlier in this book: just because God is silent does not mean He is absent. God's providence and His guiding hand are evident. He provided for Mordecai. Instead of dying on Haman's gallows, Mordecai was honored by the king. God spared him and honored him.

From Bad to Worse

Things just kept getting worse for Haman. Mordecai wouldn't bow. Haman plotted Mordecai's death. The king honored Mordecai and used Haman to do it. And the worst is yet to come. The dramatic confrontation with Esther is on the rise.

Read Esther 7:1-10.

✻ Summarize what happened in these ten verses. Don't leave out any of the juicy details!

Finally, the climax unfolds. Still recovering from his humiliating duties of honoring Mordecai, Haman went to Queen Esther's banquet as requested. There, Esther revealed the annihilation plot to her husband the king, pointing the finger straight at Haman as the man who had manipulated the king into signing the decree. Feeling enraged and betrayed by his second in command, the king left the room. Haman was terrified (wouldn't you be if you had tricked the king and been found out?), so he begged Esther to spare his life. But in doing so, as he "was falling on the couch where Esther was reclining" to beg for his life, the king walked in and saw what looked like Haman attacking Esther. Haman was as good as dead. In another twist of irony, Haman was impaled on the same gallows that he had ordered to be built for Mordecai. I cannot begin to imagine what was going through his mind as he marched up the steps of those gallows to his death. His story echoes the proverb, "Pride comes before destruction" (Prov. 16:18a).

The Hand of God

There are tons of lessons to learn from this part of the story: Esther's wisdom to wait for the right moment; Mordecai's trust that Esther would do the right thing; the destruction of the wicked. But one of the most important take-aways is this: God's hand is never far away. It may seem like the situation is hopeless, but God is always in control. He hasn't let anything slip through the cracks. Nothing happens without His knowing.

Mordecai must have wondered where God was when his life (and the lives of all of the Jews) was on the line. As an orphan living in a foreign country, Esther must have felt alone sometimes, too. That sense of isolation probably only increased when she became queen. But behind the scenes, behind the scheming and planning of Haman and the worry and grief of Mordecai, God was working.

The same God who worked in Esther's life is working in yours. Nothing in your life slips through the hands of God unnoticed. He cares for you. And He will work things out. Like Esther, you may not know why or how He is orchestrating the events around you. But rest assured, you are not forgotten. Ever.

Your Place in the Story

* From Esther's attitudes and actions in this chapter, I learned that....

* Haman's story teaches me that...

* Mordecai's life teaches me that...

* One thing I learned about God in this chapter is...

* One person I need to forgive is ...

* I really need God to work out things in this area of my life:

CHAPTER 6

Finding Resolution

IN MOST MOVIES, THE LAST FEW MINUTES ARE SPENT BRINGING RESOLUTION TO THE CONFLICT. THE COUPLE FINALLY GETS MARRIED. THE BAD GUY IS HANDCUFFED AND PUT INTO THE BACK OF A POLICE CRUISER AND DRIVEN AWAY TO JAIL. THE TEAM CELEBRATES ON THE FIELD AFTER COMING FROM BEHIND TO WIN THE CHAMPIONSHIP.

Resolution:
The point in a literary work (or movie) at which the chief dramatic complication is worked out.

In our study, the last few chapters of Esther bring a close to the story. The man who plotted the death of thousands of Jews was impaled on the gallows. Mordecai was saved. Esther successfully pleaded before the king. But what about the original decree to have all the Jews killed? Remember, a king's decree could not be revoked—even by the king himself. So how does our plot find its final ending? How are all the story lines resolved?

The New Edict
Read Esther 8:1-13.

✳ *What edict did the king send out (through Mordecai)?*

_____

_____

✳ *How did this edict solve the Jews' problem of impending annihilation? What power did this edict give the Jewish people?*

_____

_____

_____

✳ *How can you reconcile the edict allowing the Jews to defend themselves with the principle of loving your enemies?*

Since the king could not revoke his own edict, he created another one giving the Jewish people the right and authority to defend themselves against anyone trying to kill them. They could assemble together and protect themselves.

Keep in mind that Esther and Mordecai did not seek violence. It wasn't their first choice. Lives would be lost by both Jews and Persians. But this edict gave the Jews some balance, with the ability to defend and protect when faced by the horrors of injustice. Just like people stood up to the Nazis in World War II, Esther and her fellow Jews stood up against evil. They didn't seek it out, but they would not allow it to go unchecked. And the results? Check it out.

Read Esther 9:1-10.

✳ *How did the other nations feel about the Jews?*

✳ *How did the people of all the other nationalities feel about the Jews?*

✳ *What did the Jews in Susa do? More importantly, what did they NOT do?*

The Jews defended themselves. But they did not lay their hands on any of the property of those Persians who were killed in the fighting, which they could have done. This restraint and lack of greed show us that these Jews weren't just out to pick a fight. They wanted to be left alone, but they would defend themselves if they needed to. And apparently, they needed to, because Esther asked the king for permission for the Jews to defend themselves a second day (Esth. 9:13).

In the Middle

So what about you? Ever found yourself in the middle of a fight you didn't start? Perhaps someone started a rumor about you. Or a teacher accused you of cheating, but you were innocent. Maybe a bully has tormented you every day with her words or fists. Ever wonder about whether or not you should stand up for yourself or "turn the other cheek"? Here's a good thing to remember: just because you stand up for yourself doesn't mean you are being "unchristian." If someone is harming you physically or emotionally, it's OK to speak out. If you are being falsely accused, it is OK to declare your innocence. Don't be snide or rude or vengeful. Don't try to make the accuser look bad or foolish. Don't promise to get even. Just be honest and truthful and humble in what you say and do.

Time to Celebrate

The Jews were spared national disaster. Haman and his ten sons were destroyed. (See Esth. 9:10.) Mordecai was promoted to prime minister, second in command to King Ahasuerus. It was time to celebrate!

Read Esther 9:18-28.

✷ *What is the time of celebration called?*

✳ How did this time of celebration get its name?

_____

_____

_____

✳ What was to happen during this annual party?

_____

_____

_____

✳ Why were the Jews to celebrate this day every year? Why was it so important?

_____

_____

_____

The annual Feast of Purim that the Jews set forth in the Book of Esther is more than a party. It is a reminder of what God did for the Jewish people in Persia in that fateful time in history. When the Jews celebrated Purim, they were reminded that good won out over evil. That even though God was silent, He was not absent. That God was in control. That one person chose courage over fear and stood in the gap for her people. It was a way of remembering what God had done.

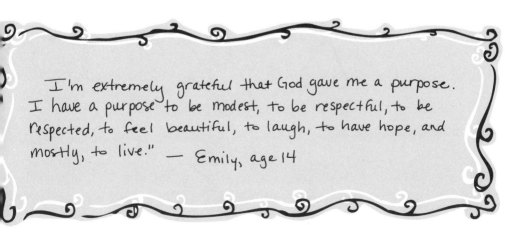

I'm extremely grateful that God gave me a purpose. I have a purpose to be modest, to be respectful, to be respected, to feel beautiful, to laugh, to have hope, and mostly, to live." — Emily, age 14

Time to Remember

✳ *The idea of remembering significant events didn't occur just in Esther. Read the following Scriptures. For each, write down the significant event to be remembered.*

Genesis 28:10-19:

Joshua 4:1-7:

Luke 22:14-20:

Jacob met God and set up an altar as a reminder of the experience. The people of Israel created a memorial as a reminder of how God had cut off the Jordan River so the people could cross over into the promised land. And most famously, Jesus told the disciples to celebrate the Lord's Supper as a reminder of His shed blood and broken body freely given for their sin. But why? Why is it so important to remember those significant moments? Because it's easy to forget. Do you want proof? Try a little exercise. In the grid below is a random combination of colors, numbers, and symbols. Study the grid for thirty seconds. Then cover the grid up with your hand and fill in the blank grid on the following page with the correct items.

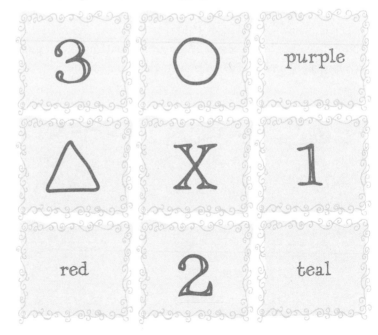

How did you fare? Did you forget more items that you thought you would? Granted, these were pretty insignificant symbols. It really doesn't matter what was in the squares. We as human beings are more likely to remember important events. Or are we?

✳ *Read Exodus 16:1-3 and Exodus 17:1-3 and find the common theme between the two stories:*

The Israelites were complaining. They feared for their lives. The scenarios were different, but the Israelites' complaint was the same: "We're gonna die out here! God has left us out in this forsaken place to perish!" So how do these two stories relate to our study?

✳ *Read Exodus 14:15-22 to review a familiar story in history. What is this significant event in the life of the Israelite people?*

Yep. You got it. The famous parting of the Red Sea. God delivered an entire nation of people from the evil Egyptians by splitting apart a massive body of water and allowing the people to pass through. With the Red Sea still in the rear-view mirror, the nation of Israel faced more challenges. And being wise people, they trusted the God who delivered them from Egypt to deliver them again, right? No, they didn't. They freaked out. Within days (two chapters in Exodus), the people forgot the miraculous and amazing things God had done for them, and they instead complained and whined that God had left them alone to die. They forgot. It's easy to forget—even the important things. That's why it's so important to find ways to remember what God has done.

In my office is a small photo frame. It's no larger than the size of a playing card. It's made of blue glass. Inside it is a simple piece of paper with the words "July 28, 1983. I was saved at Youth Camp" written on it. The handwriting is awful. The paper has yellowed with time. And yet, it is one of the most treasured things in my office. It is a reminder of where I have come from. It is a reminder of a decision that I made as a teenager that has impacted the entire course of my life. When I am discouraged and frustrated about my relationship with God, I look at that framed piece of paper. It reminds me that the same God who spoke to my heart decades ago is still working in my heart now. It encourages me when I'm tempted to give up.

Your Turn

* Do you have any mementos that mark times in your life when God worked in a special way? It could be a card, a piece of jewelry, a rock from a retreat site, a ribbon from a gift. It could be anything that reminds you of a time when God provided something for you, big or small. Write those down:

Just because you stand up for yourself doesn't mean you are being "unchristian."

Beginning to Remember

It's never too late to take the time to look back and remember what God has done in your life. In the space below is a time line of sorts. It begins when you were born. Take some time (more than just a couple of minutes) to reflect back on some significant moments in your spiritual journey—milestones, so to speak. Think about when you became a believer. A camp you attended. The death of a friend.

PRESENT

BIRTH

I was born on _____

When you're discouraged (and you will be), you can look back and be encouraged by how God has worked in your life. When you're tired (and you will be), you can look back and see how God has carried you before and will carry you again. When you're tempted to give up (and you will be), you can look back and see that the struggle is worth it. And when you are filled with joy and happiness (and you will be), you can look back and find more reasons to worship the God at the center of it all.

One Last Look

Let's take one last look at the story of Esther. It's a pretty good glimpse at a main character—but not who you might think.

Read Esther 10:1-3.

✳ *Who is highlighted in these few verses and what is said about him or her?*

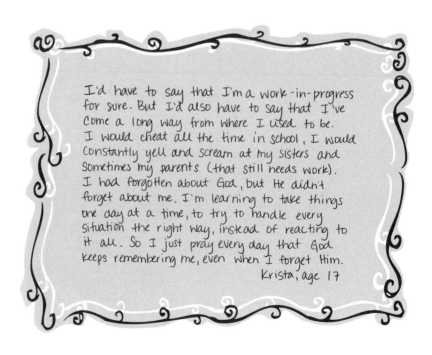

I'd have to say that I'm a work-in-progress for sure. But I'd also have to say that I've come a long way from where I used to be. I would cheat all the time in school, I would constantly yell and scream at my sisters and sometimes my parents (that still needs work). I had forgotten about God, but He didn't forget about me. I'm learning to take things one day at a time, to try to handle every situation the right way, instead of reacting to it all. So I just pray every day that God keeps remembering me, even when I forget Him.

Krista, age 17

The story of Esther doesn't begin with her, and it doesn't end with her either. It ends with an afterthought, really. The story concludes by telling us what happened to Mordecai. Funny, isn't it?

The final scene of our drama is a reminder that this story isn't ultimately about Esther, although you can learn loads from her. It's not about the king or his search for a queen. It's not even about Haman and his hatred run wild. This story is ultimately about God and His providence. It's a display of how God orchestrated the events in Mordecai's life, Esther's life, the king's life, and even in Haman's life. Throughout this entire story, God was working. And believe it or not, He was working in your life as you studied a great woman of courage.

Your Place in the Story

This study will end with you, with your life. Take some time to think about all you have learned in this study. Things you have wrestled with. Laughed at. Cried about. Still don't understand. Then compose a prayer to God. Tell Him whatever you want. Thank Him. Confess to Him. Yell at Him if you need to. Ask Him for help. Plead for Him to help someone else. Worship Him. And rest assured, He hears your prayer. Remember, even though He may be silent, He is never absent.

Teaching Helps

Keys to a Successful Small Group

Nobody wants to fail as a small group leader. In your heart, you want to create an atmosphere and experience of grace and truth. But how do you do that? If you have never led a small group before, the following tips can be helpful in creating a successful small group. If you have been leading a small group for years, allow these tips to serve as a reminder of the basics.

PICK THE RIGHT PLACE

Where you meet makes all the difference. Girls tend to be most comfortable meeting somewhere away from the church. The classroom atmosphere at church just feels too academic and confining. If possible, meet in your home. It provides a comfortable, relaxed atmosphere where girls will see you in action with your home and family. And your couch is much better than a metal chair!

SET GROUP RULES

Girls need limits, especially in a setting where personal information is shared. Make sure girls understand that what is said in your small group stays in your small group. It is not to become the latest information on the gossip grapevine. Also make sure that girls understand the importance of listening while others are talking and allowing every girl to have the chance to share. You may even need to set a time limit for discussion if you have a particularly verbal girl who tends to dominate conversation.

KEEP IN TOUCH

During the week, make phone calls, write notes, and send e-mails, IMs, and text messages. Dropping by a sporting event or special occasion will also foster a deeper relationship. Move into the 21st century and create an account on Facebook or another social networking sight so you can send short notes to them.

PRAY FOR THE GIRLS

Ask for prayer requests each week. Sticky notes and index cards are

wonderful tools on which the girls can write their prayer requests. Keep them in a convenient place so you can pray for the girls often. Make sure the requests are not left where others can see confidential information. You will learn a great deal about the girls you are leading as you read through their prayer requests. Small prayer notebooks are also a good idea for each girl to keep. They can write down each other's requests and pray for each other throughout the week. Girls love seeing someone at school who is in their small group and being reminded that they were prayed for that morning!

HOLD GIRLS ACCOUNTABLE

Teen girls need accountability in their relationship with Jesus, their relationships with others (friends, family, boys), and their emotions. That means that you must be the adult who asks the hard questions and doesn't allow girls to skirt their responsibility to themselves, God, or each other. If you see a serious issue, you need to address it. Don't worry about whether or not a girl will think you are uncool. You're supposed to be a bit uncool—you are the adult.

KEEP A SENSE OF HUMOR

Working with teen girls is serious business, but you must maintain a balance between teaching and fun. Let your hair down so they can see you act crazy at the appropriate times. Sleepovers or other fun activities are a great time to be silly and enjoy being with each other. Sometimes girls are shocked to know their leaders are real people! I remember one occasion during a Christmas party, we had a video scavenger hunt. We had to do all kinds of crazy things and make a video. We were racing to beat all of the other teams back to the church. I have never laughed so much in all my life. After that, all the girls came back to my house and spent the night. So many girls slept on my floor that I ended up sleeping under the Christmas tree. The girls couldn't believe I didn't sleep in my bed, but I didn't want to miss any of the fun. We made breakfast the next morning and lounged around until noon talking and laughing. To see me without make-up, my hair sticking up, and brownies in my teeth was just about more than they could stand!

Adapted from *Girls' Ministry Handbook* by Jimmie Davis. Used with permission.

Kick-off Meeting

OPENING

To kick off the study, create a festive atmosphere. Provide chips, drinks, etc. Allow the girls to introduce themselves if necessary. After all the girls have arrived, give each one a note card and pen or pencil. Instruct them to write on the note card some pertinent information: name, address, e-mail address, and cell phone number.

GETTING COMFORTABLE

Give girls another note card. Direct them to think of a question for someone else in the group to answer, a question that will help the group members get to know each other, such as "What was your favorite vacation as a child?" Collect cards and place them in a basket. Call on girls to pull out the cards one by one, answering the questions.

To help girls become more familiar with Esther, play a game of "Win, Lose, or Draw" or Pictionary®. In this game, everything will relate to the story of Esther. Write on separate note cards several things dealing with the story (king, queen, beauty pageant, law, feast, banquet, etc.). Group girls into teams to play. Explain the connection between the drawings and the story of Esther.

GETTING SERIOUS

Explain the importance of setting a few ground rules. Allow girls to come up with a list of boundaries, such as keeping things confidential, being honest with each other, praying for each other, and so on. As girls decide on a covenant, write it down and instruct each girl to sign it.

GET TALKING

To spark a little discussion, make the following statement and direct girls to debate its truthfulness: "Quiet women rarely make history" (author unknown). Explain that over the next few weeks, they'll discover how one person made history and changed lives. Allow girls to share prayer requests. Close in prayer. Distribute books and assign chapter 1 for next week. Afterwards, call girls who may be interested in the study but missed the first meeting.

CHAPTER 1
Teaching Plan

OPENING:

Before the session, write the following names on separate note cards: Wilma Flinstone; Hillary Clinton; Barbie; Britney Spears, Cleopatra, Beyonce', Snow White, Minnie Mouse, Madam Curie, Amelia Earhart. (You may need to add names if you have a large group.) As girls arrive, tape a name to their backs. Each girl must find out whose name is on her back by asking yes or no questions to the other girls.

TIE IN:

Say: We have begun a six-week study of an amazing woman in history. She may not be well-known in the world's eyes, but in Scripture, an entire book is named after her. Open in prayer.

REVIEW:

To review the individual study from the previous week, ask the following questions:

- What characters did you meet in your study this week? What is their role in the story so far?
- How did you do on the quiz on page 11? Do you hurry?
- When did hurrying cost you? Share a time in your own life when being in a hurry cost you.
- How can your being hasty cost someone else? *(accidents, being late with work, etc.)*
- What are some signs that our world in general is in a big hurry? *(Everything is instant—microwaves, IM, express checkouts.)*
- Which character did you relate to more this week, Ahasuerus or Vashti?
- How was being in a hurry costly in this story?
- Do you think you would have refused the king like Vashti did? Why or why not?

BIBLE STUDY:

Call on a girl to read Proverbs 19:2. **Ask:** How can being hasty cause you to mess up? Discuss responses.

Call on a girl to read Proverbs 21:5. **Ask:** How can haste lead to poverty?

Ask: What are the benefits of slowing down a little bit? What are the drawbacks?

Ask: What are some common mistakes teenagers make when they get hasty? *(cheat; make poor grades on tests; get speeding tickets; have premarital sex and possibly get pregnant; abuse steroids)*
Ask: So what do you do when you've been hasty and have made a really poor decision? What do you do then?

Call on a girl to read Psalm 51:1-12. **Ask:** What was David's sin? Does anyone remember? *(committed adultery with Bathsheba; had Bathsheba's husband killed)*
Ask: What can we learn about starting over? What does this psalm teach us? *(We need a repentant heart; God forgives; we can't make ourselves better; God's forgiveness is complete; hiding sin doesn't make it go away)*

WRAP UP:
Ask: So how can you prevent making poor and hasty decisions?
Call on a girl to read Proverbs 33:11. **Ask:** What does this verse tell us about making decisions? *(seek God's counsel)*

Call on a girl to read Proverbs 11:14. **Ask:** What does this verse tell you about making decisions? *(seek the counsel of godly people).*

Say: When making decisions, you can avoid making major mistakes by seeking God and seeking godly counsel. God's Word in James 1 tells us that God will give us wisdom if we ask for it.

SEND OUT:
Allow girls some quiet time to think of how they need to respond to this study. Encourage them to seek repentance and forgiveness for an area in which they made hasty decisions and suffered the consequences. Allow them to pray about an area in which they need God's guidance. Challenge girls to voice that desire to the other girls in the group so they can be praying for each other. Then close in a group prayer.

CHAPTER 2
Teaching Plan

OPENING:

Bring several magazines to the Bible study. After girls have arrived, group girls into pairs or groups of three. Instruct them to look through the magazines and newspapers for unexpected events that the person or persons involved didn't see coming. Distribute poster board and glue and instruct groups to create a collage of unexpected events. Allow girls to share their posters.

FUN OPTION:

Bring in several bridal magazines or prom magazines. Allow the girls to look through the magazines to choose the dress they would wear in a beauty pageant.

TIE IN:

Say: This week's study focused on the unexpected events in Esther's life. How Esther dealt with the unexpected and out-of-control events speaks volumes about her character. And we can learn a lot from her.

REVIEW:

To review the individual study from the previous week, ask the following questions:

- Have you ever had a day that started normally but ended really unexpectedly with something that you didn't see coming? (Be willing to share a time from your own life.)
- What major characters have we met in this study so far?
- What characters do we meet in this week's story?
- Describe the process Esther went through to meet the king.
- What do you think Hegai saw in Esther that pleased him so much? (Reread Esth. 2:9 if necessary.)
- What one thing stuck out to you most in this week's study?
- Based on how Esther responded to this unusual turn of events, how would you describe her?

BIBLE STUDY:

Read the following quote from Mother Teresa: "I have never had clarity. What I have always had is trust." **Ask:** How does this quote relate to our study this week?

Find some pictures of various people to show to the girls. Make sure the pictures are of people of different backgrounds, ages, races, and facial expressions. Ask girls whether or not they would trust each person. **Ask:** What makes you want to trust this person or not?

Call on a girl to read Proverbs 3:5-6. **Ask:** What is the command in these verses? What is the promise? What does God NOT promise in these verses? *(that everything will turn out perfectly)*

Call on a girl to read Romans 8:28. **Ask:** How does this verse relate to trusting God when unexpected events happen in our lives?

WRAP UP:

Share a time when you found it difficult to trust God. Help girls understand that it's OK to struggle with trust. As they mature in their relationship with God, their trust in Him will deepen.

To help girls evaluate areas they trust God (or struggle with trust), complete the following activity. Assign one side of the room as the "agree" side and the other side of the room as the "disagree" side. Explain that you will be reading a series of situations. They must move to the side of the room that indicates whether or not it would be difficult to trust God in that situation. They may choose a place on the continuum between agree and disagree to indicate their level of trust. Read the following statements:

- It would be easy for me to trust God if my dad lost his job.
- It would be easy for me to trust God if my best friend moved away.
- It would be easy for me to trust God if I didn't make the team.
- It would be easy for me to trust God if I were still single in my 30s.
- It would be easy for me to trust God if someone close to me died unexpectedly.

- It would be easy for me to trust God if my house was destroyed (in a hurricane, fire, tornado, etc.).
- It would be easy for me to trust God if I didn't receive a much-needed scholarship to college.
- It would be easy for me to trust God if I were the victim of a violent crime.
- It would be easy for me to trust God if I felt invisible.

Challenge girls to think about God's character and trustworthiness. When unexpected events come, it's important to remember that none of those things are a surprise to God. He doesn't panic. He knows what is going on even if we don't.

SEND OUT:

Prior to the lesson, create an altar area, a place where girls can meet with God. Use items that symbolize God's presence, such as a cross, a single candle, and a Bible. Also place a basket in the altar area. Distribute note cards, directing girls to complete the following sentence: "I will trust you with…" As girls complete their statements, direct them to go to the altar area and surrender their fears and commit to trust God. As they finish praying, each girl should leave her card in the basket, symbolizing a release of that issue into God's hands.

After girls have finished, close with a prayer of thanksgiving, thanking God that He is not surprised by the unexpected events in our lives.

CHAPTER 3
Teaching Plan

OPENING:

Prior to the lesson, either purchase play money or create large amounts of play money to give to girls. As they arrive, distribute money in the amount of one million dollars to each girl. Ask them to create a list of things they would do with the million dollars. Allow them to count it out and set it aside. Let them dream for a while. Then call on them to share what they'd do with the money.

TIE IN:

Ask: Did any of you choose to get rid of anybody? Did you reserve money to have someone embarrassed? Hurt? Even killed? Why not?
Say: Most of us don't carry the hurt and anger in our hearts to wish evil on another person. That just shows how warped Haman was. You learned about him this week, and we'll discuss him today.

OPTION:

Show a movie clip of someone standing up against evil or against a bully. The movie *Mean Girls* or the TV show "Gilmore Girls" will have such scenes. You could even show the "Opie and the Bully" episode of "The Andy Griffith Show." Then explain the connection to this week's study (Haman's evil plot).

REVIEW:

To review the individual study from the previous week, ask the following questions:

- How did you do on the quiz on page 37 about taking a stand? Which of those things would be easy to do? Difficult to do?
- Who were the main characters in this week's study?
- How would you describe both characters?
- What was the source of the conflict between the two of them?

- If you were to assign a percentage of the blame between the two of them for the conflict, how would you do it? *(for example, Haman was 60% at fault or Mordecai was 70% at fault)*
- How might you see this sort of conflict play out between two girls today?

BIBLE STUDY:

Ask: When you picture someone taking a stand against evil, what comes to your mind? (I picture a guy at a protest rally making a bunch of noise or a girl on the street corner with a big Bible, yelling at people that they need to repent.)

Ask: What biblical characters can you picture who took stands against evil? *(Daniel, Moses, Paul, etc.)*

When you think about those people, do you feel overwhelmed? Do you wonder if you could ever live up to their example? Why or why not? Can you take a stand against evil without being obnoxious and without acting like a fool?

Call on a girl to read 1 Peter 3:15-16. Explain that these verses give us the following tips for responding to those around us:

- Set apart Christ as Lord. He is the focus and the center of your life, not you. It's not about you and looking good or feeling good. Standing against evil is about living in such a way that others know whom you follow.
- Be gentle. Read Proverbs 15:1. Explain that a harsh, condemning response will get you nowhere. You can stand against evil by being gentle when others would be harsh.
- Be respectful. **Ask:** How can you be respectful when standing against evil?

WRAP UP:

Read the following scenarios. Direct girls to use 1 Peter 3:15-16 as a model for how they could stand against evil. Consider grouping girls into teams to come up with solutions to the following scenarios:

- Classmates are cheating on a test by memorizing answers from a stolen answer key.
- Your sister did something, and you got blamed for it.
- A bunch of popular girls are making fun of the new girl in school.
- It's prom night and everyone—including your date—is drinking heavily.

SEND OUT:

Say: It would be much easier for you and me to just go with the flow and remain silent when we see evil things happen. But think about this quote: "All that is necessary for the triumph of evil is for good men to do nothing" (Edmund Burke). Challenge girls to think about the role they play in being a voice for justice against evil in the world. Then close in prayer.

CHAPTER 4
Teaching Plan

OPENING:

List on separate note cards (one card for each girl) the following questions. (You may need to come up with other questions if you have a large group.) Explain that girls will think through what might have happened if the person hadn't done what they did. Give them paper and a pen to brainstorm an alternate ending to that piece of history if their given figure hadn't acted as they did.

- What if Rosa Parks had given up her seat on the bus?
- What if Louisa May Alcott hadn't written *Little Women*, the first piece of literature ever produced for younger girls?
- What if Jeanette Rankin, the first woman elected to Congress, had decided not to challenge the system?
- What if Elizabeth Blackwell, the first woman to get a medical degree, had chosen not to go to school?
- What if Anne Sullivan (Helen Keller's teacher) had decided not to teach?
- What if Mother Teresa had ignored the plight of the people in India?
- What if Harriet Tubman had not escaped slavery herself?
- What if Gertrude Elion had decided not to pursue a medical degree after being turned down by 15 schools? (She won the Nobel Prize for developing a drug to treat children with leukemia.)
- What if Abraham Lincoln's mom Nancy hadn't stressed the importance of reading to him?

TIE IN:

Say: Each of these women played a major role in history (either directly or indirectly) because they risked something to make a difference. Each of these women made a choice, and their choice affected thousands, maybe millions, of people. So did our main character, Esther.

REVIEW:

To review the individual study from the previous week, ask the following questions:

- What was the content of the edict that Haman tricked the king into signing?
- How did Esther find out about the edict?
- Why was going before the king such a big deal?
- Who in your life has been a Mordecai, confronting you and holding you accountable when you needed it?
- What does Esther's plan tell you about her character?
- How would you characterize Esther's emotions, thoughts, feelings, etc. in this chapter?

BIBLE STUDY:

Say: What if I told you that God wants to use you? What would you say to me? What would be your objections? What would be your fears? What would be your questions?

Call on a student to read Ephesians 2:10. **Ask:** What does this verse tell us?

Say: So if we have good works to do, what are we supposed to be doing? God has already given us many things to do.

Call on a student to read Romans 12:9-21. Distribute sheets of paper and a pen to each girl. Direct girls to call out all the things God has commanded us to do based on Romans 12:9-21 *(love sincerely; hate evil; cling to good; honor others; be joyful in hope; be patient in affliction; be faithful in prayer; share with others; be hospitable; bless; rejoice with others; weep with others; be humble; do not repay evil for evil; live at peace; don't take revenge; etc.)*

Ask: What do you think our world would be like if Christians did these things that God has called all of us to do?

WRAP UP:

Direct girls to turn their papers over and draw a seating chart of their favorite class. If it is summer, they can choose a previous semester or draw a blueprint of their home. Then label the seats (or rooms of the house) with people. Next to each person, direct girls to list one thing from Romans 12:9-18 that they can do related to that person.

Say: You have been placed where you are for a reason, for such a time as this, just like Esther. God has things for you to do and to accomplish. Don't focus so much on how God might want to use you when you graduate or when you get married or whatever. Focus on how God wants to use you where He has placed you now.

SEND OUT:
Group girls into pairs. Direct them to choose one way they will try to do the good works God has called them to do (with a specific classmate or family member) based on Romans 12. Instruct girls to pray for each other. Then close in a group prayer.

CHAPTER 5
Teaching Plan

OPENING:

Say: Sometimes fear of failure keeps us from accomplishing something. Answer each of the following statements as if fear could not enter into the equation.
- If I knew I could not fail, at school I would…
- If I knew I could not fail, in my family I would…
- If I knew I could not fail, I would talk to _____ about…
- If I knew I could not fail, one risky thing I would do is…
- If I knew I could not fail, I would try…
- If I knew I could not fail, one specific thing I would do for God is…

TIE IN:

Say: It's easy to brainstorm about what we would do if we couldn't fail. The truth is that none of us is ever guaranteed success at anything. Doing both big and small things involves risk and courage—traits Esther definitely exhibited.

REVIEW:

To review the individual study from the previous week, ask the following questions:
- Review the items on page 61. Which would be easy or difficult to do?
- Why do you think Esther went before the king so soon, even though she had a year before the edict went into effect?
- Why do you think Esther did not take the time to go through the proper protocol to see the king?
- Why do you think Esther asked for their attendance at two banquets?
- How did the final climax of the story unfold? What did Esther tell the king? What happened to Haman?
- What does this story tell you about God?

BIBLE STUDY:

Say: The story of Esther reminds us of God's providence and protection. We are reminded again and again that God is faithful. God is not off on another mission. He has not forgotten us. He is not too busy or bored with us.

Group girls into three groups and assign each group one of the following Scriptures: Psalm 18:6,16-19; Psalm 40:1-3; Matthew 10:28-31. Direct girls to draw on a poster board a picture of God based on their assigned passage. Allow girls to share their posters before asking the following questions:

Ask: What word pictures do you hear in these verses?

Ask: What do these verses tell you abut God's faithfulness?

Ask: How has God shown Himself to be faithful to you, your family, your friends, or your church?

Share a time when God was present and proved Himself faithful to you or your family.

REPLACEMENT OPTION: PAINT JOURNAL
Gather paints and brushes for each girl. Also gather some paper suitable for painting. Explain that you will be reading a passage aloud to them. As you read through Psalm 18:6,16-19 several times, girls are to paint what they hear and feel from this passage. The paintings may be a portion of the Scripture that spoke to them. It may be an abstract or very literal image. It may be one color that symbolizes an emotion. Whatever they want to paint is appropriate. After several readings (be sure to read slowly), allow girls to complete their drawings and share them with the group. Then ask the questions above.

WRAP UP:
Say: Even now, you have needs. You have areas in your life in which you need God to be faithful and providential, areas in which you need Him to be active. Distribute paper and pens to girls. Instruct them to write a letter to God, asking Him to provide in a specific area of their lives, an area in which they need to experience His faithfulness. Then, once girls have completed that prayer, instruct them to turn the paper over and write a letter as if God were responding to their request. They

can begin their letters by writing "Dear_____" and writing from there. Allow girls to share as they feel comfortable.

SEND OUT:

To close in prayer, ask girls to pray a sentence prayer, starting with "God, thank You for being faithful to..." and completing the sentence with a way God has already been faithful in the past. Then close the prayer time by thanking God for being faithful in the future as well.

CHAPTER 6
Teaching Plan

OPENING:

Before the lesson, write the following on separate slips of paper:
• The first memory I have of my mom or dad...
• The first time I threw up in public...
• The first time I went to school...
• The first time I hurt myself...
• The first time I cooked something...
• The first time I tried to swim...
• The first time I had a fight with a friend...

Put the pieces of paper in a hat. Call on one girl to draw out a slip of paper. She must answer the question and then give the piece of paper and hat to another girl. That girl must answer the question given to her and then draw another slip of paper out of the hat. She must answer that question as well. Continue the process until each girl has participated and all slips of paper have been answered.

TIE IN:

Say: Remembering is important. It gives us a sense of history, a sense of who we are. It's good to remember where we've come from and what we've learned. It's important to celebrate God's presence in all of it, which is something we learned in our study this week.

REVIEW:

To review the individual study from the previous week, ask the following:

• How did the king solve the problem with the edict to kill the Jews?
• Do you think it's OK to stand up for yourself? How does that relate to Jesus' command to turn the other cheek?
• How did you do on the test on pages 76-77? Did you discover that remembering is harder than you thought?

- Look at "Your Turn" on page 78. Do you have any mementos of times God has provided for you? (Bring in your own and talk about it at this time.)
- Take time to share the time lines from page 79.

BIBLE STUDY:

Say: One of the themes of the Book of Esther is God's providence, that even though He may seem absent, He is very much at work. Let's look at a story in the New Testament that illustrates this principle.

Read John 11:1-6,17-45. Review the story. Then ask the following:
- What was the problem?
- What were Mary and Martha's expectations of Jesus?
- How did He debunk that expectation?
- What do you think Mary and Martha were feeling and thinking? Do you think they were justified in what they were feeling?
- How did Jesus respond to their questions and emotions?
- What greater good was Jesus accomplishing? How was God's providence evident?

Say: God has a plan. In this story, He was working even though Jesus didn't answer the sisters' prayers immediately. God was doing greater things. The same applies today. God is always working, even though we may not see it. That is a major theme of the Book of Esther.

WRAP UP:

Say: One of the other things we learned about in this study was Esther's character and how God used it. Just like we learned from Esther's character, we can learn from each other's character as well.

Distribute sheets of paper and pens. Direct girls to list on the left side of the page all members of the Bible study group (except themselves), including the leader. On the right side of the page, next to each name, girls are to list one positive character trait they see in that person. It could be something they admire in that person or some trait they wish they had in their own lives. After several minutes, review the lists. Take time to discuss how God has given each person traits that can glorify God and encourage others. God wants to use them just like He used Esther.